SPARE ME:

A GUIDE TO PARENTAL PEACE

LAKING JORDAN

LIVE ON IMPACT MEDIA

SPARE ME: A GUIDE TO PARENTAL PEACE

For more information on Laking Jordan please visit: www.lakingjordan.com

ISBN: 979-8-9891468-7-1

Library of Congress Control Number: 2024916416

Cover photo: Olha Ruskykh

Published by: Live On Impact Media
www.liveonimpactmedia.com

Printed in the USA First Edition
1 2 3 4 5 6 7 8 9 10

TABLE OF CONTENTS

INTRODUCTION

This guide is meant to serve people from all walks of life because children are universal. There isn't a place where people are, that children aren't. Isn't that amazing? We all start from birth and matriculate through childhood, so some may find it interesting when they have difficulty parenting. It seems like we would understand children well having all been a child. But, that's not the case because being a child before doesn't qualify anyone to be a parent.

Parenting does take a certain amount of skill. The philosophy I have developed and chosen to parent by is the "Spare Me" philosophy. The Spare Me philosophy is a philosophy I created. In essence, it's a way of thinking that is based on the premise of self-consideration. I employ this thinking style in various roles I fulfill in my life. For this particular work, I refer to this philosophy as a parent, and I use it to keep me sane as I raise two young girls.

When you consider yourself, it sounds selfish, and it can be, especially in the wrong context. Allow me to be clear, I am a believer in Christ Jesus. I follow the teachings outlined in the Holy Bible as much as possible. With that said, Spare Me is for those parents who #1 have custody of their children full time, half time, or more than half time; #2 Spare Me is for parents who value the lives of their children and treat them as actual human beings with feelings and needs; #3 Spare Me is for parents who have fought to break generational curses and generational stereotypes and are currently striving to have the blessing of God released in their children's lives. If you cannot answer, "Yes, that's me!" to any of those questions, this is not the right book for you.

What is self-consideration in the right context? In the right context, to consider yourself is to be aware of your daily needs and wants and then orchestrate a way for them to be met.

For example, if something is bothering you such as your child yelling or whining and you want him/her to stop. The child has a need or want which is why he is yelling, but you also have a need. Your need could be peace and quiet. These two do contradict each other.

So if you do not address the issue and the child continuously screams, you are not spared. Or, if you constantly meet the needs and wants of your screaming child without ever stopping to assess how you are feeling and what you need, you are also not being spared. I like to be spared, so I find ways to address the issue, so that I can be spared. That's self-consideration, and that's the premise of the Spare Me philosophy! I hope you like to be spared! What you will also find in each chapter are some tools to help you in your life in general. Being a healthy parent starts with being a healthy person, so be prepared to be helped as a person and not just as a parent.

As you read, I may refer to specific ages for example's sake, but you are able to transpose the messages and prayers to fit the specific needs of your own children regardless of age. In addition, if you are a believer in Christ, I have included prayers after the end of each chapter to assist you in your parenting journey. These prayers will utilize language that I typically use in prayer. Blessings!

CHAPTER 1: DEFINING PROBLEM BEHAVIOR

I worked as a behavior technician for about four years. When I worked as a behavior technician, I learned the true definition of behavior. Behavior is anything anyone can do while living. The only person that does not behave is a dead person.

Sleeping is behavior. Eating is behavior. Playing is behavior. With that working knowledge, your child behaves in certain ways that you may love and other ways that you may hate or strongly dislike.

Think about the behaviors that your child engages in that grind your gears. It may be screaming, hitting, kicking, biting, thumbsucking, or talking back. Take a minute to notate some of the behaviors that you would like your child(ren) to stop.

____

____

____

____

____

____

____

Now that you've listed one or a few behaviors, imagine how life would be if your child no longer engaged in that particular behavior.

Would you be more at peace? Would you be less stressed? The behaviors that you either thought of or listed could be considered problem behaviors.

Problem behaviors are behaviors that interfere with daily living, impede growth or maturation, and heavily impact those who interact with the child. That said, all of your child's idiosyncrasies are not necessarily problem behaviors.

Some of them may be a result of their personality, and I do not encourage manipulating a child's personality as a form of parenting.

As aforementioned, I have worked in the capacity as a behavior technician and that included both in-home settings and school settings. Some of the problem behaviors I have personally encountered included hitting, disrobing or undressing, food refusal, and playing in feces or stool.

To apply the definition of problem behavior, these behaviors would need to interfere with daily living, impede growth or maturation, and heavily impact those who interact with the child daily. In these scenarios, these behaviors did all of the above.

There are other problem behaviors that behavior analysts may not classify as problem behavior because they deal with character development.

You may have noticed that your child tells lies frequently or that he is prone to avoid taking accountability.

These are problem behaviors as well. Your daughter may have a leaning toward manipulation and deceit. She may tend to pit you and her father against each other and be quite successful at that endeavor.

My philosophy on anything learned, such as lying, manipulating, and deceiving, is that it can be unlearned.

Prayer for Managing Problem Behavior

Dear Lord,
My child is engaging in some things that create difficulty for me on a daily basis (list the behavior). I'm coming to You because I know You know the origin of this behavior. In Jesus' name, I'm asking You for divine direction to manage this.

I know that I am capable and I commit to getting more understanding from You. Father, if I am antagonizing my child in any way, I repent and renounce this practice. Show me how to apologize and heal so that I can help my child heal.

I declare that this behavior will not follow them into adulthood and it must leave their life now. On days when I am overwhelmed, allow Your peace and Your Spirit to guide me. Thank you in advance. In Jesus' name, Amen.

CHAPTER 2: RULES, CONSEQUENCES & REPLACEMENT BEHAVIORS

We all have a set of internal beliefs. These beliefs, both consciously and subconsciously, form the rules of our lives. For instance, if you believe that boys are inherently stronger and more physically capable than girls, one chore you may give would be to have your son take out the trash versus having your daughter do it. That chore is based on your belief that boys are more capable of carrying heavy things. No judgment.

The question is, how can we determine our beliefs and set house rules that cause our children to adhere to them? First we need to know what we both want and don't want to see happening daily. Make a list of things you want and don't want to see.

____

____

____

____

____

____

____

Now, think about a rule that can accompany your desire. For instance, if you listed that you don't want food in your children's bedrooms. The rule would be "No eating in bedrooms". Sounds simple enough. Let's continue with another example. You may have a toddler who is going through a biting stage. The rule for your toddler would be "No biting". Again, sounds simple enough. Here is where it can become a challenge. The enforcement of the rule.

You want to make sure that the rules are enforceable and reasonable according to the type of lifestyle you live with your children. "No eating in bedrooms" is an enforceable rule, meaning you can see your child take food in his room and tell him not to, or you can enter your child's room and tell them to come out of the room and bring the food, then have them eat in the dining room or other specified eating area. This is enforceable at your house.

Where you cannot enforce this rule is at someone else's house that you do not manage. If your children spend the weekends at their dad's or with their grandparents, your rules do not apply there. Why? Because they are not enforceable there. You cannot physically be at your house and someone else's house at the same time. Therefore, the rules for your house will need only apply to your house unless someone else gives you permission to enforce the rules at their house.

Another barrier to rules being enforceable outside of location is reasonableness. Children have a sense of when rules are unreasonable, and they will challenge unreasonable rules until whomever enforced the rule is tired and worn down. An example of an extreme but also unreasonable rule for a toddler would be "Sit still" or "Don't move from this spot" without assistance. Some toddlers are capable of doing this, but remember we are talking about rules and problem behaviors.

If you have a child who does not listen when you say "stop" or "sit still" your rule is not enforceable in some way. Why does this matter? If you have a multitude of unenforceable rules, you create an atmosphere that communicates to your child that 1) you are out of control of the situation and every situation 2) you are out of options and are talking just to hear yourself speak.

If there is not a way for you to manage the rule without being constantly overwhelmed by your own demands, it is not enforceable. Any rule that you implement must be able to be enforced in some way, even if you have to tweak the timing to make it fit the standard of enforceability.

Rules are great, but children grow and change; therefore, rules have to be adjusted throughout the child's life. Instead of thinking of a ton of rules, think of principles and ideals. Ideally, what kind of children do you want to raise? Do you want them to be respectful? Productive? Kind? Giving? Wise? Good stewards? Your values are the basis and foundation of your rules. Determine what you want to see from them in their adult years and start from there.

Here are some examples of enforceable rules for a variety of age groups that tie to the ideal of respect, kindness, and stewardship:

1. No yelling or screaming at mom or dad
2. Take your plate to the sink after dinner.
3. Return items you borrowed.
4. Be in the house by 9pm in summer and spring and 7pm in fall and winter.

You can determine if you are being yelled at or screamed at, and by knowing the sound of those tones make a decision to enforce the rule. You can see whether a plate is left on the table or taken to the sink. You can determine if your child has borrowed something from a sibling and not returned it.

Finally, you can see your child return home by a certain time if he or she was out with friends. I emphasize your role in each of the rules, because your role determines if the rule is enforceable or not, which leads to the second and most important part of the process. Consequences.

Consequences

Rules are pointless without consequences. Others words for consequences are results, effects or outcomes, which can be either good or bad. People tend to think of consequences as only bad, but that's only one type of consequence. Any result is a consequence. As you determine the rules, determine the consequences that will apply if there is a violation of your rules.

Reasonable rules and reasonable consequences go hand-in-hand. As in natural laws, the punishment should fit the crime. One word to remember when issuing consequences for breaking rules is leverage. Leverage is the ability to still be able to maneuver in a given situation.

If you lose your ability to maneuver, the child will eventually have the upperhand and manipulate you and your rules. Take consequences slowly. Don't allow your anger to cause you to punish your child to the fullest severity possible for any infraction. Save the most severe consequences for the most significant violation of the rules.

Children, in my opinion, have an innate sense of what is fair and what is unfair. They also are extremely capable of manipulating situations to work in their favor. Therefore, you have to plan ahead. Issuing consequences on the spur of the moment is not usually a good idea. Your frustration levels are high and your thinking may not be clear, so it's best to have a prepared version of consequences available. This way, your child will know what to expect if the rules are broken as well.

Though you want to be prepared to issue consequences, being prepared beforehand does not have to be strenuous or thought out so far in advance. You can simply explain to your child what will happen before the rule is broken, and it prepares your child to process the course of their actions.

For example, on your way to the grocery store, your rule may be "No running in the store". This may not be an everyday rule, so your child may not be familiar with it. However, you can simply say, "No running in the store. If you run, I will sit you in the cart". The consequence for running then becomes getting sat in the cart.

An example of an unreasonable consequence would be, "If you run, I'll take all your toys away when you get home." Why is that unreasonable? The crime of running in the store after being introduced to this rule for the first time does not warrant having all toys lost. In addition, there is no immediacy of the enforcement of the consequence. The child will have to wait to have the consequence happen.

Depending on how long you take in the store and how long the car ride is back to your home, that can be an indefinite amount of time. Perhaps you decide to make an additional stop. Will you be prepared for problem behaviors to happen again, and what will be the consequence if you have already decided to take away all the child's toys for their infraction in the store? These simple steps will help keep you calm, prepared, and in control.

Otherwise, what I have observed is that the parent becomes extremely frustrated, stressed-out, and dreads the next situation where the child will need to go outside of the house with them. Therefore consequences need to have some form of immediacy.

Delayed consequences without thorough explanation will lead to confusion on the part of the child. She may forget what happened to warrant the consequence. First you, the parent, have to remember what behavior happened that deserved addressing.

In my earlier example of the grocery store, the child misbehaved at the grocery store by running. If you continue to run errands and the child misbehaves in the car and in several other places, it becomes a collection of events that you have to address later.

That can be hard to keep track of while your mind is preoccupied with other things, such as lunch or dinner or chores. Then, if you do remember each event, or perhaps even one event, you would have to go through the trouble of reminding the child what he did wrong and why he is receiving the consequence.

For the sake of clarity, waiting to issue a consequence may be warranted at times, especially with older children. However, I do not suggest this as a standard method of practice. I do recognize that there are times things that happen that cannot be addressed immediately.

Immediacy is difficult for those personalities who hate confrontation. People who tend to be a bit passive-aggressive will delay a consequence and possibly enjoy the confusion of the child about why he or she is being punished. In my own passive-aggressive way, my response to that behavior would be "Great, if your plan is to continually damage the relationship between you and your child. Delay consequences. Go for it". Immediacy is also tough for people who tend to hold grudges.

If you keep a record of things people do to you that you can then punish later, you will have difficulty implementing consequences immediately for your child. Those who value the relationship will be prepared to help their children correct the behavior by pointing it out, addressing it with a consequence, and then moving on not stewing in what happened.

As with negative consequences, you should also be immediate when issuing positive consequences, incentives, or reinforcements. When your child is doing what you asked, be immediate to give them positive feedback or verbal praises. If a child follows a rule, be prepared to immediately acknowledge that with a positive consequence, especially if it has been a particularly difficult habit for them to break. Please note that children have ways in which they feel the most loved, the same as with adults.

Pulling on the concept of love languages, children like acts of service, gifts, words of affirmation, physical touch, and quality time. Note what happens to them when you give them verbal praise, a hug or high five, spend time watching one of their shows with them, help them clean their room, or give them a gift of some sort. You can even take it a step further and ask the child what is something that you do for them that makes them feel the most loved.

As you enforce rules and consequences (positive and negative) and maintain consistency, you will notice the relationship with your child begin to strengthen over time. At first, their behavior may seem to get worse before it gets better. Behaviorists call it "extinction burst" when a child seems to ramp up a behavior that you are trying to extinguish or stop them from engaging in. This is a normal phenomenon.

Even adults increase problem behaviors before having to stop them altogether. We call it binge eating. We call it retail therapy. Most times, we engage in those behaviors if we see a need to stop the behavior. Someone might say, "I want to get it all out of my system before I stop." Some adults can identify the need to stop a behavior that is affecting them negatively, and in these cases the success of stopping will most likely be higher than in someone who is forced to stop a harmful behavior.

In both events a behavior is noted that is causing problems. For children, the behaviors that they engage in have gotten them the things they want. Therefore, when you interrupt their way of achieving success, it gets them angry, so you should teach them a replacement behavior.

Replacement Behaviors

Replacement behaviors are behaviors that do what the harmful behavior did, just in a different way. You may have a child who snatches toys from a sibling or peers at school. This is a problem behavior if it constantly leads to other children screaming and crying because their peer took something away from them. A replacement behavior would be having the child ask to play with a toy someone else is playing with. If the child doesn't get the toy he or she wants, you can have an alternate toy ready for him or her.

Sharing can be tough for little kids, but teaching your child to share early will address any selfish behaviors he or she may be likely to develop. Children have to be taught better ways to do things if the ways that they currently do them are problematic. Many replacement behaviors involve verbalizing and requesting. You may need to teach your child what to say and sometimes how to say it, even into their teenage years.

Prayer for Establishing Rules, Consequences, and Replacement Behaviors

Dear Lord,
This seems so simple in theory, but I need Your help. Where I have fear of confrontation, please deliver me. Where I have a lack of boundaries, please show me. Where I have given up, please restore me. My desire is to have more order in my home and for there to be balance and peace. I use my words to declare that there will be order in my home. There will be order in my home (say this out loud). In Jesus' name, Amen.

CHAPTER 3: GUILT-RIDDEN PARENTING

Up until this point, some parents have had a barrier wall up to receiving the methods, and it's because of this...guilt. Guilt is the feeling that you are responsible for something being terrible, someone feeling bad, or things not going well in general. Your overall mindset is that it is "your fault". You may have even been told that it's your fault for anything and everything. I want you to realize the impact of carrying guilt around as an individual and as a parent.

Assuming guilt is not the same as taking responsibility. Taking responsibility is acknowledging that your contribution affected the outcome of a situation. Being guilty is carrying the burden of outcome as solely yours. This type of feeling can cause you to be an enabler of problem behavior. The guilt may come from a variety of places. For instance, you could have decided to get a divorce and now you're a single parent.

Maybe your mom and dad were strict, and now you want to be the fun parent, but your child has become disrespectful and does not listen to authority figures. You may have to work a lot to provide, so you feel like you aren't around enough to parent. The list could go on and on, but if you feel that anything is your fault solely, you are carrying guilt around with you daily as a constant friend and companion.

Guilt is not a good friend because all it does is keep you in a state of remembering the past. You are constantly taken back to the moment you decided to do something. You are held captive to that decision and that time in your life, and when you reflect you can only see yourself and no one else. Guilt lies to you and makes you believe you were alone when you decided, in a vacuum. Like you made a choice out of thin air.

Most of the time that is furthest from the truth. There was probably a set of circumstances that led you to make a decision. You could have even been very clear-headed at the time, but because things may not have turned out the way you hoped, you now feel guilty. Guilt does show that you have taken responsibility, but what it also does is make you over assume the responsibility. You own the entire situation and the outcome, and that is not fair to you. Since guilt is already causing you to replay the situation in your head multiple times, the next time it happens, look again and see who else was involved. What else was involved?

I'm not suggesting that you blame other people for a decision you made. I am suggesting that you acknowledge any other roles involved in your decision making and give them responsibility for the outcome as well. You are not taking it off of you and putting it on someone else, you're breaking free of the lie that you acted selfishly and in solitude with no offending factors. You are sharing responsibility.

What happens when you have raised your children and you feel the damage is already done? As parents, our job includes nurturing our child, caring for his physical and emotional needs, advocating for his well-being in the event that it is threatened in any way, thus keeping the child safe. That's the natural side of it. We also have spiritual components to raising children if we are believers in Christ.

Sometimes, all of these responsibilities can take a toll on us and something might go undone. We may have the tendency to be frustrated, yell, cry, and even hide from our children at times. We may have put a significant other before our child and that relationship did not work out. I personally know people who have given their children to other family members for them to raise while they keep living their lives totally free from the responsibility of parenting.

No judgment. We all have made decisions that we don't feel the most proud of in retrospect. Those feelings of failure in seasons of parenting, can cause us to feel guilty.

Should we have done better in any particular season? Possibly. However, the past is the past. There is no going back to undo any damage that was done. We can, on the other hand, acknowledge the damage we have done and the pain we have caused. Then we should let it go. Another thing we can do is give ourselves grace as we reflect on our decisions.

We ought not to excuse our bad behavior, but we should keep it in perspective. How old were you when you made the decision you made? Who influenced you? Do you see any particular pattern in your past behavior? These are questions we may not be able to answer alone, and it may be beneficial to explore them with a trained professional such as a therapist. Sometimes our behavior is deeply rooted, and we do not know the origin point or we think we have healed past it, so we refuse to take even one single look at what happened in our past. If you find yourself speeding past a particular time in your life regarding your parenting or how you were toward your children at a certain time, I encourage you to stop.

Slow down. Make yourself walk through that season mentally and examine it closely. If you can remember the damage you did to your children, you can most likely remember other circumstances surrounding your behavior.

Finally, if things need to be addressed with your child directly, address him or her. Allow him to fully vent or explain what life was like during those seasons and try not to interrupt. Again, you may need a family therapy session for deep work such as this. Seek wise counsel. Pray and let the Holy Spirit lead you in how to handle the situation. We cannot control the narrative that our children will have or the light they will choose to see us in. Therefore, we do the best we can and we let God do the rest. He is capable of correcting any misunderstandings our children have about the way they were raised. He is not holding our mistakes in parenting over our heads, but our mistakes should admonish us to be gracious to others in their mistakes, even our children.

Ok. You have acknowledged that you carry guilt which has caused you to under-parent, but you also realize you still have time to correct the behavior because your child is still young enough to be molded. What is the next step? Brace for impact. Your mind has now shifted from being a pacifier to being an enforcer. This is a new you. Your child needs to be introduced to this version of you.

The pushover is gone. You may ask, is it that simple? It is simple to stop accepting the guilt of your past decisions, but it takes time to reframe your thoughts and to understand why it is important that you do. You can't just drop bad habits overnight. This takes conscious effort.

Sit down and write out your daily schedule. Identify the areas where you previously operated in guilt. It could be after school at snack time or at dinner time when you acquiesce to your child's demands and screams that she be able to get dessert before dinner. You may have a food trauma story that you remember that you are projecting onto your child, and it keeps you giving in to them not eating what you have prepared for dinner.

Ask yourself, who is being punished more in the situation where you have to prepare six different meals to meet the demands of your family because you feel guilty about making food your children don't like. I am not suggesting that you give them gross food that they hate everyday, but the reality of life is that things don't always go the way we want, and some nights a parent may be overstimulated from the day and needs additional rest.

If your children are conditioned to getting whatever they request because you feel guilty about making food they don't like, it will be hard to accept the feelings of rejection. You have to deal with the feelings of them being unpleased, which is difficult for those who struggle with people-pleasing.

Guilt-ridden parenting can cause you to be overworked mentally and sometimes physically. We did decide to give birth or agree for a partner to give birth to a child in order to become parents. No, a child did not ask to come here. Nevertheless, that does not give a child the right to be demanding, unappreciative, and manipulative toward their parents.

Parents are stewards and guardians. Good parents are good stewards and guardians. That is enough. When you see that you are extended beyond your capacity, look at where you are feeling guilty and address that issue within. Have a conversation with your child, no matter the age, and let the child know that changes will be taking place. Then follow through. There are very few things worse in parenting than giving a speech about making changes, and then not following through. We will address the impact of lack of follow through later. Or will we?

Prayer for Freedom from Guilt

Dear Lord,
I hand you this burden of guilt. I can no longer carry it, and You said for me to cast my cares on you for you care for me. I confess that there is trauma attached to the guilt that I feel. I repent for honoring the trauma by carrying guilt. I acknowledge the trauma, but I do not have to honor it, respect it, or give it the privilege to control me anymore. All guilt related to trauma must leave my life now. Your assignment is up and your consequences canceled, in Jesus' name, Amen.

CHAPTER 4: FOLLOW-THROUGH

The step on following through is one of the most critical steps in helping with a behavior change. I can recall a time as a registered behavior technician where a parent gave me a seemingly specific rule she wanted me to enforce.

I understood that there was a boundary that she didn't want her child to cross, and if he crossed that boundary, he would receive the loss of a privilege. It seemed pretty straight-forward to me. I believe the child understood, and as we proceeded to play and the boundary came into our view.

I held firm on what the parent communicated. The child violated the boundary, and I took away the privilege. However, her response to the way things transpired puzzled me. She acted surprised to know that the privilege was revoked and she proceeded to pacify her crying child as if I did something harmful to him.

I did not expect that response under the assumption that she gave me a directive, and I followed through. As I finished my notes that day, I wondered if she did not expect me to follow through. I questioned myself about what went wrong. The consequence wasn't unreasonable in proportion to the rule. What happened in my experience is that because the consequence was invoked and it produced a sad response in the child, the parent felt guilty. This is a sort of reverse psychology. The behavior of the child elicited the consequence. He violated the boundary, thus he in effect chose the consequence. If I had not followed through with what his mom told me to do, I would have communicated two things.

One being I didn't care what his mom said, and two he shouldn't either. Neither of which I could comply with. Needless to say, I tried to communicate extremely clearly on subsequent visits about her rule. It did not get better.

Follow through or lack thereof is a louder communicator than some understand. When you set a rule or boundary and it is violated, you are responsible for step two, which is administering consequences. Is it frustrating to have a rule broken when you explicitly reviewed the expectations? Yes. It is. However it is also equally, if not more, frustrating to constantly have your rules broken and boundaries violated. The goal in these situations is for you to have parental peace. You cannot ignore the breaking of rules and boundaries because it affects you internally. You can tell yourself that it really doesn't matter, but what you are really saying is I don't believe I can get the respect I need or demand and there is nothing I can do about it. This is untrue.

Your establishing of consequences is a step in the direction of doing something about being disrespected, but a further and more pronounced step is following through on your consequences. Either way, whether you follow through or not, you are teaching someone how to treat you. People, children included, are not obligated to give you anything you don't require. When rules are violated and boundaries crossed, it is not a time for hugs and kisses. There is a time for that, but it is not at the time when you have to enforce the rules and give consequences.

If you have developed a habit of not following through, you can change that today. Acknowledge that you have had a pattern, and even reflect on where or when that pattern developed. If you journal, find some time to write about it.

Once you've completed the task of acknowledging, change your mind to be that of a person who no longer accepts rule violations and boundary crossings with no repercussions. Your relationship with your child will change from one of disrespect to one of respect. Please also understand that affection does not replace follow-through.

You can discipline your child and give them affection afterwards. Some parents dole out affection instead of discipline and reason that hugs or kisses makes a child want to do what they've asked. No amount of hugs and kisses will change your child's perception of you if you don't follow through. Change may not happen overnight, but with time and consistency it will happen. In the worst case scenario, if your child does not change, you will still have changed, and the peace that you desire as a parent will be more attainable than you first thought possible.

Prayer for Help with Following Through

Dear Heavenly Father,
I acknowledge that I have allowed myself to be run over. I have laid down as though a doormat. Today, I confess that that was wrong of me because it allowed my inner peace and self-worth to be diminished. I come boldly requesting Your help in following through. I have been a people-pleaser, and internally I have told myself that I cannot stand to make my children or others uncomfortable, and that I should rather suffer with the discomfort instead.

I now disagree with my previous beliefs and practices. I have rights as a parent and as a person. I can set rules and boundaries, give consequences, and follow through if those rules and boundaries are broken or violated. This is my right. Even if my child or another person disagrees with my rights, that does not negate my rights. Now Lord, please steel me against the pushback I could receive for following through. As I gain a new sense of self-worth, help me to love who I am becoming. In Jesus' name.

CHAPTER 5: HOME–SCHOOL CONNECTION (UNDERSTANDING AUTHORITY)

Up until this point, you may have felt like you're doing well with parenting at home, but your problem with your child shows up mostly when you send them to school. First let me submit to you that these principles of Spare Me extend beyond parenting and into any sector where the primary job is to work with children. Therefore, teachers, daycare workers, pediatric doctors and nurses, occupational therapists, speech therapists, and the list goes on should use these principles in their work with children.

Why do I insist? Children are expert loophole finders. In my opinion, they are adept at noting who practices issuing rules and consequences and following through. They recognize people who walk in authority quite quickly. I'd even go as far as to say, it is spiritual. Ponder that.

We often see it in homes where the father is a masculine and dominant figure. The children may take a while to follow mom's instructions, but when dad speaks there is almost an immediate recognition that he is serious. This can also not be true due to the father relinquishing his responsibilities and his authority as well. However, in a general sense children tend to recognize those with authority.

Having God-given authority or innate authority is a benefit, but it can cause those who don't understand principles to be frustrated when they meet a child who has rebellious tendencies. These types of children do not recognize any form of authority. You may find them in the principal's office often, or in juvenile detention centers. They may walk the streets without adult supervision and speak harshly about police officers and respectable professionals.

They don't tend to see the difference between themselves as a child and the adults that they encounter. In their minds, they are on the same level in life as the adult addressing them. This type of thinking can stem from several different causes. When a parental figure has left or abandoned a child, the child could have developed a disrespect for adults. When an adult has belittled or berated a child often in anger, the child will lose respect for the adult. When an adult has abused a child physically, mentally, emotionally, or sexually, a child will no longer recognize the authority any other adults have. Hence, if you are a parent or parental figure, and you are privy to any of these instances being the case, this could explain the poor behavior between a child and his teachers as well.

Behind-the-scenes in school

I have matriculated through several levels of public education as a teacher. I use the term matriculated because I started on one level, and I have made it to higher levels relative to how I manage my classroom. When I started out as a 23-year-old college graduate with zero years of experience, I expected students to simply "listen" to me. I did well with building relationships, but my lack of setting boundaries affected my ability to manage my classroom.

I used incentives, but they were arbitrary. I tried anger, but that wasn't my style, thus it didn't work. I also had difficulty planning lessons, so that affected my ability to manage my classroom as well.

My experience is not unique, and this is not to bash teachers or give difficult students an excuse for their behavior. A teacher's years of experience should not automatically classify them as unable to manage classroom behavior. Though I started out rough, I have observed several first-year teachers who were able to control the most unruly of students.

What matters more than experience is understanding your authority as the teacher, being direct and clear about classroom rules and consequences, and following through. Those are the principles I've been mentioning.

When your child is acting out at school, when you find out about the issue, it becomes your responsibility and role to act as an advocate. For whom do you advocate? Hear the issue out, and determine if the rules of the school have been broken.

Whether your child was justified in breaking a rule or not, you are on the wrong side of right if you advocate for your child breaking a school rule. This includes classroom rules. Rules are generally in place to maintain a safe and orderly environment. In our society, we have rules of the road and laws of the land that govern public behavior.

There is a caveat. If the rules of the school are in any way discriminatory, that becomes an issue you need to face on a higher level than that of the classroom teacher. The rules of the classroom should be clear, and any contact you receive should be to address the breaking of rules or the violation of consequences. If your child receives a consequence at school for an offense, it behooves you to also give a consequence at home.

Is this a double punishment? If you choose to see it as that, yes it is. I choose to see it as Spare Me philosophy. By your child getting in trouble and you having to be contacted at work or during your day, that does not spare you. When you have to show up for parent-teacher conferences to discuss behavior and hear the things that have been happening in the classroom, that does not spare you.

Therefore, if you choose to leave the school behavior unaddressed at home, the school will continue to have to involve you in what's going on. Remember, ultimately this is your child and you are most responsible for your child. The solidarity that you show between yourself and the school will allow your child to see that he cannot continue to wreak havoc at school and nothing happens at home.

On the other hand, you may be in support of the teacher and the school, yet your child is still having difficulty. I strongly encourage you to advocate for your child in this instance. What I hate to see is a student being mistreated and no one seems to believe him or care that it is happening. That will cause the child to mistrust adults and to expect other teachers subsequently to be untrustworthy as well.

I've spent more time than I realize repairing the teacher-student relationship due to some teachers having personal biases and the student knowing and understanding that he hasn't been treated fairly.

The home-school connection is a double-edged sword to some degree. However, if you pray about things, pray about it first before you start making any decisions. You know your child, but you may not know your child when you put him in the midst of 20+ other students. Some students thrive in front of an audience. This is where you get your class clowns.

They were designed by God to entertain, and they get their practice in the classroom. I've also worked with students who have manipulative tendencies. They love to work the school and the parents against each other. It's a chess game of sorts for the child, signifying that he has found weaknesses in both his parents and his teachers in terms of how they handle discipline.

Whoever supports the child the most in this instance is his advocate, and he will exploit the advocacy and create further division in the relationship between the adults. You may also see this happen in a co-parenting situation as well. Finally, in terms of the home-school connection, recognize your own school trauma. Memory can be a tricky thing. Sometimes we remember things exactly as they happened, and sometimes we only remember the feeling a situation created for us. Your experience in school may be directly affecting your child if you have unhealed trauma that happened at the hands of a teacher or an administrator.

Your school years are some of the most formative years of your life. If your experience was laden with you being unsuccessful academically or you being labeled anything that caused you to be insulted daily, you may feel that a teacher is responsible. You may be right, but be sure not to project your negative experiences onto your child. Children emulate their parents, and when you share stories of how "bad" you were in school, it gives your child something to connect with, especially if you have very little in common with them otherwise.

Be aware of your triggers and traumas from your schooling years, then make a conscious effort to avoid addressing your child's issues in school as though you are reliving your own issues. Your child is different from you no matter how similar you two are. The time period in which your child is attending school is different from the time period in which you went to school. You are not the child, and the child is not you.

Prayer for the Home-School Connection

Heavenly Father,
I have had some difficulty with ________________'s behavior at school. Show me the root cause. If it is lack of follow through at home, show me. If it is lack of follow through at school, show me. I am here ready and willing to get instruction on the best way to steward ____________________'s life. I am willing to start all over in how I have handled things that happened with him at school previously. Please strengthen me as I take on this endeavor. In Jesus' name, Amen.

CHAPTER 6: HOME-WORLD CONNECTION

We spent the last chapter diving into how home and school need to be connected for the implementation of Spare Me. Now we will look at the connection between home and world. The ironic part of this equation is that if you have a school-aged child, school is her world. However, your child may be involved in extracurricular activities such as karate, gymnastics, music lessons etc. that occur in the world, outside of the home, but they may directly affect the home.

When it comes to other areas of your child's life besides school, there are generally other adults present in his life that contribute to his development. When it comes to these areas, you don't have the direct influence on your child that you generally have due to them being in someone else's care.

In these instances, you want to be spared as well. Remember that there are specific rules and consequences that you implement in your home and in your presence that you cannot implement in other settings. How do you circumvent problem behavior or plan to address problem behavior when you are not there to address it? You teach character development and you discipline when there is poor character.

When we started this journey, I mentioned that you want to nail down what type of person you want to send into the world. Do you want your child to be respectful? Kind? Bold? Demonstrative? What do you ultimately want to emphasize in her character that you expect her to demonstrate when she is out of your presence? Where some parents falter is, they see character traits and flaws in their children and they assume that those traits are a part of their personality and nothing can be done to change that.

This is partially true, but it is not an absolute truth. You may find that your child has a bend toward dishonesty. Many parents find this to be true, but they stop short of disciplining dishonest behavior. When you discover a deficit in character, your child's ability to behave with high ethical and moral standards, you have a responsibility to address it because this is the individual you are sending into the world. Your child is essentially an adult in a small form. The ways in which he thinks and behaves or operates will carry him into adulthood.

If left unchecked, the child will carry selfish ways, manipulative ways, and disrespectful ways into adulthood. As the parent, you have to teach character development and discipline. Choose two to three ethical and moral behaviors that you want your child to exhibit. List them below:

____

____

____

When your child is out of your presence, you can still hold her accountable to the character you want her to develop. For instance, if your daughter goes to cheer practice, her coach should expect her to be a leader but to also treat others with respect and kindness.

If she does not do that, the coach should be able to address her, about how that went. In the beginning, it can be a conversation if she is being rude or unkind to her peers, but if the behavior continues, you can implement a rule and a consequence simply because you are not being spared.

First-then rule

There is a principle in the world of behavior called The Premack Principle. Some call it the first-then rule. Essentially, you present this rule as a prerequisite to what your child wants. It works for all ages. You tell your child what you want to see first or what you want to happen first, and what you are willing to do for them as a follow-up later. You need leverage to use this rule.

Your child may want to go somewhere. You can say to your child, "First a day of practice without a negative report, then you can go to your friend's house." This puts him in a position of control over whether or not he will earn the opportunity and it shows you as the parent whether or not your child understands what is expected of him outside of your presence. Please hear this loudly and clearly. All you need is one time to determine if your child understands your expectation no matter how old your child is or if he or she has special needs. When your child meets your expectations at least once, the precedent has clearly been set in their minds and should be set in yours. You have to grab hold to that one time and lock it in your permanent memory bank.

This will help you in times when your child may gaslight you or make you feel like he can't do something that he has clearly shown you he can do at least once. As with everything, there can be some caveats. Some children with special needs do have regression as a symptom of their disability. However, if regression is not a typical symptom, a parent should not assume that the child is in a state of regression.

If you need to keep a journal of the things your child has shown you that he can do, keep a journal. Accountability is a part of character development. I have worked with many children at a variety of ages and maturity development. It pains me to see when a child has been so effective at manipulating their parents and other surroundings because he has not been held accountable for his character. Children who don't have the character to treat people well as children will not develop this character spontaneously as adults. Make the connection between home and world by teaching your child character development and disciplining when you see that he is not learning what you are teaching. Remember consistency and follow through are just as key in this endeavor as in any other behavior endeavor.

Prayer for home-world connection

Heavenly Father, I know what type of person I want my child to be, but what is most important is what type of person You want him to be. Help my desires to align with your desires for him, and give me courage to address any character flaws I see in love. I need courage to discipline those flaws. Please forgive me for blaming these flaws on his father or grandmother or anyone else. I take responsibility for allowing my child to behave in poor character ways. I repent for thinking that other people should straighten him out when it has been my responsibility from the beginning. I will continue to pray for my child in this area. In Jesus' name, Amen.

CHAPTER 7: REWARDS & POSITIVE REINFORCEMENT

In chapter two, I mentioned consequences, which included positive consequences as well. In the world of behavior specialists and analysts, positive does not mean good. It means more or to add to as in addition. Consequently, negative does not mean bad; it means to take away from or decrease.

If you think of it as integers, positive and negative numbers, that can possibly help you understand the jargon of a behavior analyst. An example of positive reinforcement could not be a good situation at all.

This is where I see some people struggle to understand how behavior works, and it is my delight to help them understand as clearly as possible.

If you want more of a behavior, you reinforce it positively. You focus on it. You incentivize it. You make it a big deal. Then you get more of it. Sounds simple right? However, where parents get confused is when they have been reinforcing a behavior they don't want more of and they wonder why it keeps happening. It is simply because you are focusing on it; you're incentivizing it, and you're making it a big deal. This is how a child learns to manipulate a parent.

A tantrum, for instance, is not birthed out of a situation where a child is unsure of what the results will be. A child enters a tantrum fully aware that the likelihood that it will end in them achieving their goal is very high.

This happens partly because the child has received what he or she wanted as a result of that behavior before, so to increase the odds of getting their needs met, they increase the intensity and duration of the tantrum.

This is not always the case, because we also have to know the motivation of the child before we can determine why the tantrum is happening. This is simply one example of positive reinforcement that is not necessarily a positive feeling. Another example of positive reinforcement is for those who like words of affirmation. If you compliment a person on something he or she did, said, or wore to work one day, the likelihood that the person repeats the action, phrase, or outfit is higher than if you did not acknowledge said person. When you want more of a behavior, you reinforce it by adding the response the person is looking for.

This may not always be your intent, but if you examine situations closely where you are getting more of behavior you both want and don't want, you will see that your attention is closely tied to the outcome.

There is an old saying that goes, "You win more flies with honey than with vinegar". The implication there is that sweetness is better than sourness.

When you focus heavily on punishment, it makes situations intense, and it takes away the hope that your child or spouse or anyone working with you may have. It is difficult to work with, live with, and be around someone who is constantly negative and finding the worst in every situation.

It weighs on your spirit to be around someone who constantly grumbles and complains. The same is true for children. They enjoy the presence of other children, especially children who are carefree and positive.

That said, you should spend time teaching your child the principles of life and disciplining them, but you should also spend time recognizing the good that he does.

You may not have grown up in a home where the parents recognized any good that the children did, but that does not have to be how you raise your children. You can point out when they made good choices, or when they did a kind deed. If you feel like your child is not capable of doing anything kind or good, I encourage you to take a look at yourself and your reflection.

Many times the child you have is a reflection of either you, their environment, or both. This is a harsh truth, but acceptance is one of the first steps to getting on the right track. Let's pray.

Prayer for help with positive reinforcement and rewards

Dear Lord, I need help with my speech. I have had a tendency to see the glass as half-empty instead of half-full. Please help me change my perspective from a negative perspective to a positive perspective. You said in Your word that life and death are in the power of the tongue. I want to speak life over my child and not death. I declare now that I will speak about the good my child does; I will speak positively about the efforts my child makes. I will build my child up and not tear him down as often as I am conscious of it. In Jesus' mighty name I pray, Amen.

CHAPTER 8: CAREGIVING & INDEPENDENCE

All parents should start off with a heavy amount of caregiving for their child. Your infant needs you throughout the day and night to feed her, wash her, change her diapers, burp her, carry her around, brush her hair, and everything else that she cannot do in her tiny infant body. Infants cannot sit up for quite a while.

They cannot crawl and it takes several months for them to learn to hold a bottle. Furthermore, they are around one-year-old or 12 months old when they start demonstrating the ability to stand without support, indicating that walking will soon take place.

These milestones happen in the lives of typically developing children. There are developmentally appropriate milestones that childcare workers, interventionists, and medical workers use to assess whether or not a child is progressing at the appropriate rate.

In healthy child-parent dynamics, the goal is for the baby to gradually take on more responsibility. This is not simply a cultural idea or what some would consider based on western ideals. Most babies begin to assert their independence by trying to roll over, pulling pacifiers out of their mouths, kicking socks off, and a variety of other things to let you know they want to have some control of something in their tiny lives.

I've worked as an early interventionist and a registered behavior technician (RBT). In my work as an early interventionist, I assessed infants and children and scored where they landed developmentally. It was clear to see when a child was not making the progress expected of them by a certain age.

In my work as an RBT, I encountered children with autism daily and many of their goals centered around independent living. They needed to learn the things that neurotypical children learn, such as shoe tying, washing dishes, brushing teeth, and how to make their beds.

Both of these career fields involved caregiving and independence. In my opinion, the most successful clients and families are those who recognize the need for support as soon as possible and they get that support regardless of any stigma associated with it. In addition, successful families don't limit a child and relegate them to only what they see them do.

They have a healthy amount of encouragement that includes urging the child on to reach goals that he might otherwise refuse to meet. This is not a one-size-fits-all approach, and strong encouragement and urging may not work for all children.

I do advocate for encouraging and urging a child to do hard things because life can be hard, so teaching them how to encounter difficult situations at home can prepare them for when they will face them outside of home.

If your child has special needs, it may take them longer to learn a skill or concept. Determine what would "spare you" if your child could do it. Then make a plan to have the child learn the skill and reinforce him when he accomplishes it until it is time to move on and learn something new. Your child may take longer to learn something; however, it is not the length of time it takes to learn it that matters most.

What matters most is your child's sense of autonomy and the quality of life you start to have as a result of teaching them how to do things on their own.

Look back on what your child has accomplished from infancy until now. Is she walking? Is she sitting up? Is he going to the potty or indicating that he has gone? Is he putting on his shoes or socks without assistance?

Take a look at what she has accomplished and think back to how it happened. It didn't happen by chance. It happened by choice, either yours or hers. The same holds true as your child ages. Nothing changes. The only thing that should change is your child's ability and your perspective.

Chores

At what age should your son or daughter begin doing chores? I refer you to the "Spare Me" philosophy. What chores would spare you if your child did them well? The key word is well. One of the first tasks we teach toddlers that spares us as parents is potty training. We teach them to go to the potty because it becomes obvious that the child knows what is happening with his body when it's time to pee or poop.

This is evident by the child hiding to poop. This is evident by the child verbally saying "I'm wet" or even making demands such as "change me". The same is true for other chores.

If your child can make a complaint about something in the home that needs doing, she can probably do it herself. The complaint in itself is recognition of there being a need. Let me be clear, I am not advocating for children to take on all adult tasks to spare you as the parent.

Reasonable chores such as loading the dishwasher, vacuuming, cleaning the bathroom, and doing laundry are all things that a child can do for him or herself probably starting in late elementary and early middle school. You also don't want to have a child doing so much housework that she cannot have a childhood.

Another consideration with chores is having older children take care of younger children. Making an older sibling do things for the younger siblings may spare you, but that is not the siblings' child to care for. In this instance, I would encourage parents to ask for help from the older siblings rather than requiring the older siblings to perform parental duties.

If asking is too liberal of a concept, I encourage the parent to communicate that he or she needs help with a task rather than making it solely the responsibility of the older sibling. You could theoretically give an older sibling a chore of helping a younger sibling get dressed, or pack a snack, something light and simple.

The lines get blurred when the older child is expected to care for the younger child as if he is the younger child's parent. Again, a child should be able to do chores yet have a childhood.

In their early years, children do not necessarily need to be relegated to gender roles for chores. A son can wash dishes as well as a daughter. A daughter can take trash out as well as a son. You may think to yourself that you want to teach your son or daughter what to expect in a spouse, but that is erroneously assuming that he or she will 100 percent get married and moreover, married to a person who wants to do the things that he or she did not learn to do or were not required to do growing up. In my opinion, it is wiser to teach your child to do all the things that need to be done in a household because as an adult he may have to do them.

Before I move forward, I must address the killer of independence, and that is codependency. When you have a problem with codependency as a parent, you are a danger to your child. This means that you do not want to see him succeed apart from you because then the child will no longer need you, and you need to be needed.

Please understand that this is a toxic course of action, and it will breed resentment and rejection later in your life with your child. If he becomes aware that you are a hindrance to his growth in any way, he may not want to be in close relationship with you or have his future children around you later in his life. Making people dependent on you is an unhealthy way to cultivate relationships. Therapy may be needed for you to understand why you are finding ways to sabotage your child's growth. Take a close look at your behavior as a parent, and ask the hard question. Am I codependent on my child? Do I use her need for me to validate me as a parent or as a person? Am I angry when he learns to do things that don't require my interference?

Watching your child grow up and being sad that he is no longer a baby and doesn't need you that much anymore is normal. Sabotaging his relationships with others and stifling his ability to achieve any of his goals without your help is toxic. You'll find a prayer with language that addresses codependency.

In the next chapter we will discuss parenting adults.

Prayer for Caregiving and independence

Heavenly Father,

I have hit a juncture. I see my child growing and changing and I want to let her do that, but it is hard. I realize that if I hold on too tightly, I will impede her growth. I need help yielding and giving her to You. I don't give her to the world. I give her to You. You know the plans you have for her life. I repent for holding on to my child as though You were not capable of protecting her.

I repent for the throne I placed myself on in her life. I voluntarily step down now and let You take Your rightful position. As she grows and develops, show her how to be independent the way You want her to be. Please don't let her have an insecure independence that screams I don't need anybody, but let her have a true independence that trusts Your plan and Your way for her life.

For any way that I have come into agreement with delay in my child's life because of how I have been in the way, I repent and I am sorry. In Jesus' name I pray. Amen.

CHAPTER 9: PARENTING ADULTS

Is there such a thing as parenting adults? The answer to that question would depend on a few factors. Is your adult child living at home with you? Does he or she have exceptional or special needs?

If your adult child is capable of making decisions, no matter how great or poor those decisions, you should no longer be parenting that adult. When you have a child or multiple, you become a parent for the rest of the child's life; however, parenting is a practice not an identity.

Adults are assumed to be grown ups who can work, handle important responsibilities, and make decisions aware that the outcomes may or may not be in their favor. This is what distinguishes children from adults. Children are typically unaware of the possibilities and outcomes of a given situation.

They have shortsightedness due to being youthful. It is not a flaw, it is simply a design of children to be child-like. When you treat your adult child as though he is incapable of making decisions, you are affecting your relationship with him adversely.

As a parent, if your adult child has been typically developing with no cognitive delays, you have had her entire childhood to teach her the things that she should know and use in her adult life. If she is an adult, she has already determined her worldview. No amount of parenting will change her mind. Only life experiences will serve as teachers now.

This may not sit well with parents who like to be overly involved in their child's life. You have had time to train and teach that child. If you are still trying to train and teach an adult, you are fearful that if you let the child go either physically or metaphorically, you have not done enough for that child to be successful in life.

That is a you problem. That is not your child's problem.

When you insist on parenting an adult, you will most likely get negative feedback from that adult. Another consideration for you is to release any residual parental guilt you may be holding on to. There is no rewind. There are things that we reflect on and would change if we could; nevertheless, most of those things could involve people we no longer have access to.

Those people, that job, those relationships have evolved into something different, and we had to accept this evolution and change because time moved on and we lost access.

The same is true for your child. He has evolved into an adult. Though you still have access to him, that is not a license for you to continue to parent beyond the boundaries that adults need.

Boundaries

Your adult child may live at home. In this case, I suggest boundaries and not rules. Telling your adult child what time to be in the house is ludicrous.

You can have a healthy conversation about what boundaries you would like to set so that you are not disturbed whenever he does come in, but house rules for adults can be insulting. The "my house, my rules" philosophy needs to be abandoned when your child reaches adulthood. You might say, "Well, he needs to get his own place then." If you feel so strongly about your adult child not living with you, set a timeline and have a discussion.

What I have seen is that parents enjoy having their adult children live with them because it gives them a sense that their child is safe under their watchful eye. The proximity gives them access into the adult child's life, and keeps them relevant to the child to control them in some way. There may be healthy adult child/parent relationships where they cohabitate and get along great, but I would advise a close examination and inspection into the health of that situation.

Some of the more religious readers may allude to the Bible in that it says to honor your mother and father so that your days may be long on the earth. Honor does not mean to submit to everything your parents tell you to do. In that instance, your child would be putting you in the place of God. That, as I mentioned in the last chapter, is a recipe for codependency.

Be sure that you are not using the term "honor" as a form of manipulation and control. If your child chooses to take a different route than the route you suggested, is that dishonorable or is it adulting?

You may be wiser. You may have walked a path that you see your child walking, and you know how it ended for you. You may have credence to feel how you feel, but when you intervene before your child gets to experience life, you rob her of the learning experience.

Note that allowing your adult child to disrespect you is never an option. Again, determine the boundaries of the adult child/parent relationship, and insist that they not be crossed. Keeping in mind that your adult child also has boundaries that you should not cross. Things can get hairy if you have allowed your child to see you being mistreated, abused, and misused at the hands of your lover or spouse, but you then demand respect from the adult child.

If you have not required respect from other adults in his presence, when the child becomes an adult, he will be convinced that he also has reached a level in which he no longer has to respect you either.

In addition to the Spare Me philosophy, another of my philosophies is that parents should become friends of their adult children. Friends give advice, but they do not insist that the advice is followed. Friends listen sometimes with and without giving a solution to a friend's problems. Friends are hands-off unless they are requested to be involved in some way. You won't be friends in every sense of the word, but the relationship dynamic will be healthier if you become a friend to your adult child rather than trying to parent the adult.

Not all adult child/parent relationships can result in friendship due to abuse and other significant traumatic issues that arose in childhood. However, if it is possible to maintain relationship, parents should back off from parenting their adult child and see that adult child as their equal. Afterall, in the world at large, that adult child has all the same rights as you, the parent.

Prayer for Parenting Adults

Dear Lord, my role as parent has extended into my child's adult life. I pray that I will be able to see my child as an equal. You gave my child to me to steward until adulthood. I have completed that task. My child will still need me and my advice from time-to-time, but I pray that You will help me to guide him and not to parent him. Every document that my child needs to be a full adult including her birth certificate and social security card, I will give to her. I want to leave her well equipped for life when it is time for me to depart this phase of eternity. Bring to my remembrance anything that I need to give him or show him for him to be as successful an adult as possible. In Jesus' name. Amen.

CHAPTER 10: LOVE VS. ANGER & CONTROL

Love is a central and most important component of parenting and disciplining in parenting. Parenting devoid of love is like having a house without a roof. There is no protection there from the elements.

Nothing inside the house will be useful if it is always being rained or snowed on. There will be damaged items that don't serve a useful purpose anymore. Though the house may have once been furnished with beautiful and expensive pieces, if they are damaged and scorched by the sun or hit by lightning, the beauty will diminish and even completely vanish so that what was once there is no longer able to be remembered. The purpose of a roof is to cover and protect what's inside the house. How are you covering and protecting your child today?

Love according to the Bible includes discipline, and you can read about that in Hebrews 12. In fact, God explains when you don't receive discipline it is the same as being rejected and disregarded. Those we love, we discipline. We don't control however. What is the difference?

Control comes from a place of anger. Discipline comes from a place of love. When your child makes you angry, you can find yourself plotting against them in your mind. Those plans might include how you can make their evening difficult. You might go so far as to torture your child in a variety of ways and some of those ways may even borderline on emotional, mental, and physical abuse.

This behavior comes from wanting to control the child. On the other hand, when you discipline out of love, you calm down from your anger and begin to think rationally.

Some questions you may find that you ask yourself in these moments are, why is he behaving this way? Is there something I did not communicate well? If I don't address this now, what will it look like in the future?

These types of questions are solutions-oriented. These questions are insightful. Love spurs others on to do better. Does your reaction to your child spur him on to want to be better or are you releasing frustration, anger, and resentment?

I recall a time when I worked for a tough boss. She had many dictator-like qualities. Dictators like to wield power over others. They like to see people squirm under their hand of control. When dictators see people thriving, they seek to snuff out their joy and success. Her leadership style was full of control, and it in-turn made people angry. Though you may gain a level of submission, the undercurrent of the hearts of those you lead is rebellion.

Someone is waiting for an opportunity to overthrow you and rebel against you. This can be true of your parenting as well. When you make yourself offensive to your child because you are so controlling, you are aiding in him having a rebellious heart and nature.

Isn't it your job to teach your child right from wrong? It absolutely is, but measure your heart and motives as you do this. If you are a Christian parent, your job is to lead your child to Christ and allow the child to make a decision to accept Christ as his Savior. Your job is not to make a replica of you because that is not what God intended.

A Different type of love

Sometimes parents can smother-love their children. In these instances, children end up not being able to function properly in adulthood. The parent has overly coddled and excessively helped the child. We see this played out later in romantic relationships.

Sometimes a mother has shielded and protected her son from various forms of discomfort, and when he is interested in a monogamous relationship, his partner discovers that he is inadequate in contributing to the household. The same can be true if a girl child is excessively spoiled throughout her life. When this happens, we see a man looking for a woman who is a replica of his mother and a woman looking for a man who is a replica of her father.

Smother-love is a form of fear. It suggests that if you step away from being so determined to see your child succeed or to keep them from getting hurt, the child will fail beyond repair. This leaves no confidence in the child, and he can feel the lack of confidence coming from his parents.

In Chapter 3, we discussed guilt-ridden parenting. Your style of protection may be warranted and valid if you were abused; but that does not mean it is not detrimental to the development of the child.

Take a moment to speak this aloud, "I am not my child, and my child is not me". This is a truth that, when accepted, can free you from feeling as though you can give your child exactly everything you did not have.

The truth is, because you grew up during a different time period and you lived through a different set of circumstances, your child actually may not need everything you needed when you were growing up.

Living vicariously through your child can be both selfish and manipulative if you are using your child to right your wrongs, take your missed opportunities, and make you feel better as a person. For any child, that is a lot of responsibility to place on their shoulders.

As a result of this, some children feel as though they are not living, and some have even taken their own lives to escape the burden of carrying the disappointments placed on them by their families. Additionally, some have disconnected from the family unit to obtain autonomy and a sense of freedom from their controlling and smothering parents and parental figures.

On the flipside, some parents have disconnected from their child because the child refused to allow the manipulation and control, disguised as love, to dominate her life any longer.

In both scenarios, being transparent, honest, and willing to receive critical feedback could help the situation if not fix it. If any of the descriptions mentioned resonate with you or remind you of your parents or child seek out a qualified therapist.

There are undoubtedly wounds and trauma that need to be addressed in these relationships. Sometimes these issues can be addressed in a group setting. Other times, you may find that you need to seek counseling individually for personal growth and accountability. Let's pray.

Prayer to Discipline from love and not control

Heavenly Father,
The way I have conducted myself as a parent is troubling. I can see clearly now that it was not just my child who was the problem. I have had impure thoughts toward my child. I have desired to control him in more instances than I can clearly remember, but I choose to repent for my actions today. I choose to accept that I have acted in a way that does not speak faith in my child but rather doubt.

If the relationship is beyond repair Lord, I ask that I be able to communicate my remorse and allow my daughter to move on peacefully. If it is not, I pray for reconciliation. I commit to allowing the Holy Spirit to help me change my behavior. If I do not change, I recognize that my child is not obligated to do more than honor me by being respectful. I renounce the false belief that my child owes me something. She owes me nothing. I release her from my expectations of repayment in Jesus' name. Amen.

CHAPTER 11: THE POWER OF PARENTAL WORDS

There was a time when I faced a serious bout of depression. I couldn't seem to pull myself out of it, and honestly I don't think I realized what I was battling. A once dear friend of mine sent me a book from a well-known minister. The book was about hope and not losing hope. I realized then that I had been fighting despair as well, which is a form of hopelessness. The author strongly emphasized the power of our words.

See, I had always identified myself as a glass half-empty kind of thinker. In my opinion, it was better to be realistic than optimistic. In my culture, we call it "keeping it real". In my effort to not lie to myself about my reality, I left little possibility for hope. When you focus solely on what you can see, you cancel out all possibility that things can improve in any way.

What further seals the deal is when you open your mouth and begin to profess only what you see. Why is this such a major issue? Simply put, whether you believe in the Bible as God's Holy word or not, it is a mentally healthier option to be positive and speak positively. The Bible says in Proverbs 23, As a man thinks in his heart, so is he. It also says, the power of death and life are in the tongue and they who love it will eat the fruit thereof in Proverbs 16.

There are other sayings, such as "If you believe you can achieve it" and "Your attitude determines your altitude". Along the road of life, some people have realized that by declaring what you have instead of what you see yourself having is like wanting a fresh vegetable garden but refusing to plant any seeds. How can you possibly see the manifestation of fresh vegetables but you haven't planted any seeds? This also takes me into the principle of reaping and sowing.

Reaping and sowing

Think of your words as seeds and the atmosphere that catches them as the ground. What are you putting into the ground that will sprout up later? Words are powerful. The Bible even speaks of how difficult it is to tame the tongue in James 3. It is nearly impossible to reign in your speech. When we are reckless with our words, it is as if someone has given us grenades and we are launching them wherever we choose regardless of what damage they cause when they detonate. The same is true of when you speak death and curses over your children. You may have even had death and curses spoken over you, so you are perpetuating your childhood experience. However, you can stop that pattern today.

I got free of depression when I dared to hope. Not only did I hope, but I consciously worked to speak positively about my life and my situation. It was not easy because for years I had learned to "speak my mind" and most of those times, I didn't care who felt any particular way about it, especially if I deemed it to be true. Now, I am guarded with my speech. I realize that my words carry power.

I don't throw out hurtful words to damage people when I am angry. Do I feel like doing that sometimes? Absolutely, and I'm certain I could do quite well. Below the belt would be my specialty.

I realize that I could plant words that will result in a crop of devastation and destruction in another person's life whether the person can hear me or not because that is how word curses work. But I know that God would not be pleased with that behavior, those evil words, or those word curses. I would also have to give an account to Him when I stand before Him. God cares about His children, adult children but also actual small children. He does not want us to lead them astray with our words. He does not want us to destroy them and put them down with our words.

One possibly overlooked way we use our words recklessly is when we lie, and some parents lie to their children frequently. The power of your word matters; your word in this instance being your agreement to do or not do a planned activity. For instance, you may have promised your child a toy or a game of some sort when times were good and there was no reason to feel you couldn't fulfill your promise.

Let's say, an unexpected expense comes up and now you have to use those funds for what came up thus inhibiting your ability to fulfill the promise you made. That is not your child's fault, and he or she should not have to suffer disappointment because of what came up. I am not advocating for neglecting your responsibilities in the face of difficult circumstances, but I am asking you to be aware of your parental practices. Is this something that happens often? Do you miscalculate what you can afford to do? Do you throw around ideas about vacations and extravagant plans that you end up not following through with? Remember chapter four was all about follow through.

Some parents have the most difficulty with their children because the child has deemed the parent to be unreliable and untrustworthy. And rightfully so if you continuously renege on your agreements. Keeping your word should be especially monitored carefully in co-parenting situations. In these situations, oftentimes a parent who is not the custodial parent makes a promise that he or she may not adequately be able to fulfill for a number of reasons.

When the plan falls through on the adult's end, the adult has the ability to reason through the scenarios that caused the plan to fail. Children don't have the same ability. Children don't understand priorities well. They don't have to understand priorities because that's the beauty of being a child. Adults should understand priorities. Therefore, I encourage the use of "loose language" when making an agreement with a child. When I speak to my children about plans I use terms such as "we may be able to do this" or "I plan on it, but I am not sure" or I specifically say "I'll try but I cannot promise you that".

This type of language does not create a definite image in the child's head nor does it signify 100 percent certainty of any particular plan. This is not to keep myself from being held accountable.

The intent of the "loose language" is to help my children to understand that changes happen that are out of my control, and rather than have them be mad and disappointed afterward, I prepare them beforehand for any changes. I would rather surprise them with something they had hoped for by following through with it though I may have used "loose language" than to use definite language and make promises that I am unsure I can keep or fulfill. It may seem like a small matter in the grand scheme of things, but you are teaching your child what to expect of you and others when you either break promises or keep them.

In Proverbs 3, King Solomon told his son to write God's words on the tablets of his heart. I can almost guarantee that you currently have words written on the tablets of your heart that were hurtful, false, mean, degrading, upsetting, and unsettling. But do you have words on your heart that build you up, encourage you, strengthen you, settle you, and give you peace?

You may not have had those life-giving words spoken to you, but you can speak them to your child. It will make you vulnerable, but your vulnerability will breathe life into your child, their children, and their children's children. And if you haven't had those words spoken to your heart, you may have to speak them to your own heart.

Practice speaking positively in the next few days, weeks, and months. You will see your perspective shift from what can't be done to what can be done. You will see your hope rise. You will see yourself change from being a Negative Nancy or Negative Neal to a Positive Patricia or Positive Paul. Once you change your thinking and speaking you will begin to easily hear the negativity that other people speak over themselves, their lives, and their children.

You may already be thinking and speaking positively, and your urge may be to stop a negative-speaking person right away and correct them. That's one way to do it, but put yourself in that person's shoes before you employ that method. The person may be in deep depression and cannot see how these little but powerful changes may help him. In that case, prayer is probably going to be your best option.

Speak positively about the negative-speaking person and believe that he will be able to use his words for edification and not destruction.

If you have found that you struggle with managing your tongue, we can pray about it, so let's pray:

Prayer for Managing the Tongue

Heavenly Father, I am guilty of using my words to tear down more than I have used them to build up. I am guilty of finding the most hurtful things to say to people who have upset me. My tongue has been my greatest weapon. I lay my weapon down today, but I am asking you not to leave me defenseless. When I want to revert to saying harsh things, give me the strength to overcome. When I cannot find something positive to say, help me redirect my thoughts to things I can be thankful for.

Give me a tongue of gratitude. Show me how to create a life that glorifies you by simply changing the way I speak. I need your help today with my words and my speech God. I am using my words now to say, Father please help me. In Jesus' name. Amen.

ADDENDUM: SPANKING–PHYSICAL DISCIPLINE

Should you spank your child? This is a debatable topic amongst people, not just Christians. Here is my definition of spanking: using your hand or some flat object to hit or paddle your child on the rear-end, bottom, buttocks, arms, or legs more than once. I choose not to use the term "whoop" or "whooping" when referring to spanking due to the connotations it has with the enslavement of Black Americans. I also choose not to use objects that are related to whips to physically discipline my children for the same reason.

The Bible is clear in stating that if you hit your child with a rod, he will not die. The actual scripture is Do not withhold correction from a child. If you strike him with a rod, he will not die Proverbs 23:13 (TLV). That said, spanking is a physical discipline that a parent may or may not be comfortable with. In no way do I condone, whipping with an extension cord or anything hard enough that can leave indentations on the skin, broken skin, excessive bruising or the like.

Weigh your motives. Do you intend to hurt your child or teach them? Sometimes the two can coincide if you are angry. Your thought process might sound like, "I'm going to teach them a lesson" or "You will learn today" as you plan out how you will inflict punishment on your child. However, the big question is do you have other methods of discipline? This is a question for both parents who spank and who chose not to spank.

For parents who choose to spank, how often do you employ this tactic? If it is daily and there is no decrease in the behavior, it is ineffective. Remember the chapter on rewards & positive consequences. There is also the age of the child to consider. Getting a spanking at certain ages is embarrassing due to the emotional, hormonal, and developmental changes a child may be experiencing. Have a conversation with your child about what form of discipline he or she learns the most from.

You might find that the child does fear spankings more than anything, and sometimes the threat of a spanking with the right wording, will correct behavior. However, if a child says, "Spankings don't really hurt" or "I just get it over with and go back to doing what I was doing", believe them.

Spankings are not a long-term solution as it adds an immediate response but does not always serve as a reminder of what to do should the situation arise again. Oftentimes, the situation does arise again.

As a parent, do you spank everytime the situation arises? Again, if the behavior has not changed, the punishment was ineffective. Please also consider the laws in your state regarding physical discipline. If the laws in your state are not in favor of corporal punishment, follow the laws of the land. Whichever decision you make, strive for the most inner peace that you can attain, and more importantly strive for peace that remains.

Made in the USA
Columbia, SC
21 April 2025